Violence at School

Perspectives on Violence

by Gus Gedatus

Consultant:
Dr. Michael Obsatz
Associate Professor of Sociology
Macalester College, St. Paul, Minnesota

LifeMatters
an imprint of Capstone Press
Mankato, Minnesota

LifeMatters Books are published by Capstone Press
PO Box 669 • 151 Good Counsel Drive • Mankato, Minnesota 56002
http://www.capstone-press.com

Printed in the United States of America

Library of Congress Cataloging-in-Publication Data

Gedatus, Gustav Mark.
      Violence at school / by Gus Gedatus.
          p.   cm. — (Perspectives on violence)
      Includes bibliographical references and index.
      Summary: Discusses different types of violence that occurs in schools, causes of these actions, their effects, as well as possible solutions to violent behavior.
      ISBN 0-7368-0422-6 (book) — ISBN 0-7368-0439-0 (series)
      1. School violence—United States—Juvenile literature. [1. School violence. 2. Violence.] I. Title.
      LB3013.3.G43 2000
      371.7′82—dc21   99-048462
                                                 CIP

Staff Credits

Anne Heller, Charles Pederson, editors; Adam Lazar, designer; Heidi Schoof, Jodi Theisen, photo researchers

Photo Credits

Cover: Stock Market/©Jose L. Pelaez, large; PNI/©Ken Wagner, small
FPG/©Ron Chapple, 44
Index Stock Photography/12, 32, 35
International Stock/©Phyllis Picardi, 50; ©Scott Barrow, 53, 54, 57
Photo Network/©Grace Davies, 10; ©Myrleen Ferguson Cate, 59
Unicorn/©Eric R. Berndt, 6; ©Jeff Greenberg, 27
Uniphoto/©Bob Daemmrich, 16, 23, 37; ©Mark Reinstein, 46
Visuals Unlimited/©Tom Edwards, 9

A 0 9 8 7 6 5 4 3 2 1

Table of Contents

Chapter
Overview

Chapter Overview

Almost three million violent crimes take place in or near American schools each year.

Violence is words or actions that hurt people or the things that people care about.

Bullies often seek to lower other students' self-esteem. Threats against students or teachers can lead to physical violence.

Thefts and vandalism are forms of violence that are common in schools.

Weapons are becoming more of a threat to safety in schools.

Chapter 1

The Different Kinds of Violence at School

You might have heard about violence in school. You might even know someone who has experienced it. It may seem like some schools have a lot of violence against students and adults. In fact, about 2.7 million violent crimes take place each year in or near American schools. That is about one violent incident in a school somewhere every six seconds. The figure includes fights, injuries, and killings. The figure also includes violence that is not physical, like theft and vandalism. Vandalism is needless destruction of others' property. These figures are serious.

However, school is still one of the safest places for kids to be. For some people, school may be safer than their neighborhood or even their home. Shootings like those at Columbine High School in Littleton, Colorado, in 1999 are extremely rare. Fewer than 1 percent of students are killed at school. Still, we all can do things to make ourselves safer. This book will discuss some of these ways.

Bill was the shortest guy in his class. He didn't think it was any big deal. Everyone in his family was short.

BILL, AGE 15

When Bill entered ninth grade, a new guy named Nathan was in his class. Nathan was much taller than Bill. Nathan was always hanging around with lots of other guys. He seemed popular. He started calling Bill "Shrimp." Nathan's friends thought that was funny.

Bill didn't think Nathan would ever start pushing him around or hurting him, but he wasn't sure. Bill tried to avoid Nathan but usually saw him anyway. He began to feel a little afraid of Nathan. Bill dreaded school because of his fear of Nathan.

Myth: School crime is directly related to racial mix.

Fact: Recent reports show students' race or ethnicity has had little to do with the incidence of crime in school.

The Definition of Violence

Violence is words or actions that hurt people or things they care about. It can be as simple as a threat or as deadly as murder. Nathan's insults were verbal violence. Bill was never shoved, punched, or wounded. However, Nathan's verbal violence hurt the way Bill thought about himself while he was at school. Nathan was bullying Bill, a common kind of violence at school. The words stimulated Bill's fear of physical violence. The words encouraged his fear to grow.

Violence changes the way people feel about their space, which includes their privacy, rights, and freedom. It can cause them to be less trusting of others. It can make them feel afraid, anxious, nervous, and confused.

This chapter describes some of the common types of violence in school. These include bullying, verbal threats, theft, vandalism, and the use of weapons. It also looks at ways fear and spreading rumors can lead to violence.

One in three American high school students has witnessed a physical attack at school. Out of each 100 students ages 12 through 18, 12 students have been victims of a physical attack, bullying, or robbery.

Bullying

Bullies are people who pick on others. They know they can humiliate, or shame and put down, their victims. They want to show power or superiority. From early childhood, many people have to deal with the threat of violence from a bully. More than half of all U.S. students have been bullied themselves or know someone who has been.

Some experts believe that bullies have unusually high self-esteem. Others believe bullies may have extremely low self-esteem. In any case, bullies usually enjoy lowering the self-esteem of others and dominating them.

Threats and Physical Violence

Many students make threats about or to other people. Though these threats may hurt, most never lead to physical harm. In some cases, however, they do. A violent response to a verbal insult may be immediate, or it may occur some time later. People may react on impulse. Acting on impulse can cause sensible people to do foolish things. For example, some people believe the shooters in Littleton were reacting with violence to put-downs they had received.

Sometimes people follow through with fights after they are insulted simply because they have an audience. Fear of ridicule, such as being called chicken, can cause disputes to mount. First comes the insult, then the shove, and then the punch.

Violence can affect teachers, too. Their main job is to educate students. They also want to keep order. This can lead to threats of violence against them.

Theft and Vandalism

Theft is the most common form of school crime. Thefts in schools often go unreported to police. School authorities may handle the problem if victims report the stealing. Sometimes the thief is a person the victim knows. For example, someone steals an article of clothing or a book from another person's locker. If the victim accuses the thief, the victim may face a fight with the thief.

When a person steals something from someone he or she knows, the victim faces additional dangers. The victim may be able to identify the thief. Then the victim may worry that the thief will try to keep him or her from saying anything. Or, the victim might not pursue charges against the thief. Such silence may encourage the thief to rob the victim again.

Vandalism is a kind of stealing as well. It may involve graffiti, which wrecks school property. Graffitti is drawing or writing on a public surface. Vandalism may involve destruction of school equipment or other property. No matter how you look at it, vandalism is violence that should be reported.

Weapons in Schools

The use of weapons in school disputes is growing in America, especially in the inner city. The most common weapon among students involved in school violence is a knife or blade. Sometimes students carry guns.

Homicide, or killing someone, is the most serious form of violence. From 1992 through 1994, there were 85 homicides in U.S. schools. Guns caused all but four of the deaths. It is true that 85 deaths is a lot. However, in the same period, there were about 147 million students in U.S. schools. The great majority of students did not directly see or feel the effects of weapons in school.

Experts talk about the Three F's to reduce violence at school: family, friends, and faith. What do you think these are? How can you get them or help others find them? How do you think they reduce school violence?

Rumors That Lead to Violence

If you don't want to be a part of violence, it's important to be careful about what you say. Sometimes people can make explosive situations worse by discussing them. For instance, two people are having a conflict. Through rumors, you may hear an accusation that one supposedly made about the other. The rumor continues until the accused person hears the comment. Then the accused person's anger increases. You may be adding fuel to an already fiery conflict if you repeat the accusation to anyone.

When you hear threats of harm to a person, tell someone who can help rather than telling your friends. Such conversations among friends often are nothing more than gossip. By repeating negative messages to someone else, you are likely to do more harm than good.

Whenever Angela heard some gossip about someone else, she

repeated it. If she overheard a threat against someone, she made sure that person heard about it. Often she thought she was helping people. Angela loved it when people called her "The Source."

Several fights occurred because Angela repeated something unkind. She was always careful not to get involved. After all, she thought it was never anything she had said that started fights. She was only passing on what she had heard.

Angela never slugged or pushed anyone. She never took anything that didn't belong to her. She never carried a weapon. However, Angela was indirectly but deeply involved in lots of violence.

Violence at School

Points to Consider

What is your definition of violence?

If you saw a close friend being bullied, what would you do?

What would you do if you heard of a plan for some violent activity? Who could you tell?

What would you say to someone like Angela who contributes to violence by spreading rumors?

Chapter
Overview

Sha over apter orvie

School violence has been a growing concern.

For some years, the rate of theft and assault in schools rose. Today, the numbers are lower.

School violence has grown in small towns and suburbs as well as in big inner-city schools.

Multiple murders took place in eight schools during an 18-month period in the late 1990s.

Chapter 2

A History of School Violence

When Marla was younger, she found out that her father had

MARLA, AGE 16

been injured in high school. Some guys had cut him with a switchblade. He hadn't done anything wrong. These boys were trying to steal his portable radio. Marla's dad had to go to the hospital for stitches.

Marla's dad joked about getting his name in the paper. He said that happened because when he was a student, back in the early 1970s, stabbings in schools were uncommon.

Marla has never been involved in any fights in school. She tries to keep to herself. When she senses that people around her are stirring up trouble, she goes somewhere else. She never forgets what happened to her dad.

A Changing Problem

For years, violence in schools has been a concern. School misbehavior once involved things like being late, chewing gum, or talking out of turn. Over time, misbehavior grew from vandalism to physical violence against people. The fistfights of the 1950s escalated, or increased, into confrontations with weapons in the 1970s. Theft and assault became more of a threat to school safety. Assault is harming someone physically. An increase in the use of alcohol and other drugs added to the problem. People think less clearly when they use such chemicals.

From the 1970s, the rates of both minor and serious theft and assault increased. School violence grew in small towns and suburbs as well as in large cities. Students' fears have grown along with this increase. Some fears, however, may arise from increasing numbers of news reports that focus on school violence. The reports make it seem as if violence is everywhere. That is not true. Research shows that schools are still among the safest places for young people to be.

The number of young people charged with criminal offenses in Canada decreased from 150,665 in 1993 to 121,122 in 1997. That's about a 20-percent drop.

For several years, the number of students who regularly carried weapons increased. Recently, the number of guns found at U.S. schools dropped 30 percent.

Bullying remains the number one type of violence in schools. It is also one of the most overlooked. Chapter 6 talks about ways to deal with bullying and other kinds of violence.

Recent Events

In the last half of the 1990s, young people committed over a dozen multiple homicides in U.S. schools. Consider the following events from late 1997 through early 1999. As you do, remember that in 1998, there were about 90,000 public schools in the United States. That is an occurrence of homicide in one out of every 6,000 schools. Violence in schools is real. Such extreme violence as homicide is extremely rare.

"Ever since I was a kid, we've had guns in the house. They're all unloaded, have trigger locks, and are locked in a gun cabinet. If you have guns in the house, at least put trigger locks on them. They're only a few dollars. They can save lives if there are kids around who might pick up the gun and play with it."—Jamie, age 17

October 1997, Pearl, Mississippi—A 16-year-old killed his mother and two classmates and wounded seven others.

December 1997, West Paducah, Kentucky—A 14-year-old killed three students and wounded five others. In the same month in Stamps, Arkansas, a 14-year-old killed two classmates.

March 1998, Jonesboro, Arkansas—A 13-year-old and an 11-year-old killed four classmates and a teacher. They wounded 10 others.

April 1998, Edinboro, Pennsylvania—A 14-year-old killed a teacher and wounded three students at a school dance.

May 1998, Springfield, Oregon—A 15-year-old killed a student and his parents and wounded 23.

June 1998, Richmond, Virginia—A 14-year-old wounded a teacher and a school aide.

April 1999, Littleton, Colorado—Two teens, an 18-year-old and a 17-year-old, killed 12 students, 1 teacher, and then themselves. Twenty-eight people were wounded.

Masud moved to the United
States from Africa when he was
13. He learned English quickly and made good friends,
especially through the school golf team. He liked his school.
Nothing worse happened than someone pushing or yelling at
another person. As Masud grew older, though, he became
increasingly fearful of violence on the school campus.

"My family left my country because of the killing there,"
Masud said. "We came to America for its opportunities and
freedom. I didn't think I would worry for my safety here. But
I worry almost as much as I did in my home country." Masud
decided to do something about the way he felt. He thought he
must be able to make his school safer.

Points to Consider

Do you think being a student was easier in the 1950s than it
is now? Why?

What do you think might happen if someone at your school
carried a weapon?

What could you say to someone who fears violence at
school?

What would you tell Masud to do to make his school safer?
How would that help?

Chapter Overview

Peer pressure, revenge, and crowding in schools can influence the amount of violence.

Guns and other weapons are more available to teens than ever before.

Some people learn violent behavior at home beginning when they are very young.

Some violence in schools may be related to alcohol and other drug use.

The media carry many false messages that may influence violence.

Chapter 3

Causes of School Violence

Some teens grow up without positive role models. That means they don't have someone who shows them an example of positive behavior. Some teens might not learn how to be happy and productive. They might not know how to solve conflicts peacefully. Other young people may have low self-esteem. They may have difficulty managing such feelings as rejection or disappointment. They just may not fit in. These feelings sometimes result in anger, which can lead to violence.

In the 1993–1994 school year, 52 young people were killed in U.S. schools. The numbers dropped in 1995 and even more in 1996 and 1997.

Influences on Violence

Peer pressure can greatly influence school violence. Peer pressure occurs when people encourage a certain behavior in a member of their group. Peer pressure can be positive, as when peers help others settle an argument without a fight. Sometimes peer pressure is negative and can increase school violence. For example, peers may encourage a fight at school by cheering it on.

Sometimes violence in one school influences similar acts in another school. This is called copycat violence. It appears to be copied from someone else's acts. Some schools have avoided copycat violence because officials watched for it. For example, in 1999, several students in Cleveland, Ohio, seemed to be planning to copy the Columbine shootings. School officials learned of the plan and stopped it before anything more serious happened.

Experts have found that people who have been victims of violence are more likely to use violence. This use of violence may occur out of revenge, anger, or fear. For example, if someone is bullied, he or she is more likely to bully someone else. If young people can experience less violence, then hopefully, their participation in violence also may decline.

Crowding in Schools

Some schools are more likely than others to have problems with violence. One reason for this tendency may be overcrowding. The teacher-to-student ratio is usually low in large, crowded schools. Students often don't get enough individual attention. They may feel that teachers overlook or neglect them.

In many schools, portable classrooms have been added. This arrangement tends to complicate traffic flow between classes. It may break down communication among teachers. Students in these settings sometimes feel confused or annoyed. These situations may contribute to school violence.

The Availability of Guns

Today it is easy for some youths to get guns. Young people may sneak guns from home and bring them to school. Teens can purchase different types of guns on the street. Anyone with enough money, including students, often can buy guns at low cost.

Students carry a gun for many reasons. Peers may have dared them to bring one. Students may carry a gun because they believe it will protect them. They might want to feel cool, powerful, or in control.

Any weapon can seriously hurt someone. Guns are especially dangerous. Someone who is angry or scared is more likely to use a gun.

GARRET, AGE 18

Since Garret was little, he saw violence at home. Garret's mother and father often hit or yelled at each other. They also yelled at Garret and his brother, Daniel.

If Garret tried to stop his parents, they reacted harshly. Eventually, he quit trying to stop them, but anger grew inside of him. He couldn't show his anger at home, so he showed it at school. He bullied smaller kids. He got into fistfights. He began to carry a weapon to feel more powerful. Finally, he bought a gun. "No one's going to push me around anymore," he told Daniel.

Violence at Home

Some people who have committed violent acts in schools grew up in homes where violence occurred. Nearly all violent juvenile offenders were physically, sexually, or emotionally abused. Much of this abuse occurred at home. When parents put down one another or their children, it has a negative effect. Some parents shove or punch each other. Children may learn that violence is an acceptable way to deal with a problem. For example, Garret learned from his parents that abusing someone smaller is okay.

In some homes, children learn to be bullies. They may be encouraged to fight if someone opposes them. Parents even may promote the belief that only cowards walk away from a fight. Bullying might be one way to feel in control. It is likely that this behavior will be used at school.

Not all young people who grow up in violent homes become violent themselves. Some can resist the effects of violence. This ability to resist is called resilience. These young poeple may have positive role models outside of their home, such as teachers or friends. They may be successful in sports, the arts, or hobbies. Some have friends who support them in positive ways. Such support helps students build self-esteem.

Alcohol and Other Drugs

A large number of violent incidents every year involve the use of alcohol and other drugs. Not everyone who drinks will choose to act violently. However, people who use alcohol and other drugs have less control over their angry impulses. Using drugs makes it hard for a person to think clearly. It can make protecting oneself difficult. It can cause people to act in ways they would not otherwise act.

Some violent incidents in schools relate to buying or selling of drugs. Drug deals may involve a lot of money. For example, the violence may stem from misunderstandings about the money. A person involved in a drug deal may fear being exposed to authorities.

The best way to be safe is to avoid places and events in which you know alcohol or other drugs are present. If you can't avoid the situation, then get away as soon as you can.

The Influence of the Media

People see many false messages in TV, newspapers, movies, music, and video games. For instance, these media often show that it is manly to carry a weapon. They may give the message that only cowards walk away from a fight. The media may show that sexual violence against females is okay and common. They often show that using guns and drugs is acceptable. They may show that whoever is best at hurting or killing others will be the winner.

Some people already see violence in their homes or neighborhoods. Violence shown in the media more strongly influences these people. When people see only violent solutions to problems, they are less likely to learn peaceful problem solving.

Myth: Once people have learned violent behavior, they can't change.

Fact: Violent behavior is learned. It can be unlearned through positive coping skills and effective management of anger.

Here are some other ways in which viewers, listeners, and readers of the media may be influenced:

They may be desensitized to, or become less affected by, violence because they have seen so much of it.

They don't learn nonviolent ways to solve problems.

They start to think violence is a normal, acceptable way to deal with conflict.

They learn that desirable things can be obtained through aggression and violence, often without punishment.

They learn that sexual violence is okay.

Points to Consider

What do you think about teens having guns at school?

What are some ways that children may learn violence at home?

What are some ways using alcohol or other drugs can lead to violence in school?

If you were a parent, would you control the amount of television your child watched? Why or why not?

Do you think TV, music, or video games contribute to violent behavior? Why or why not?

Chapter Overview

Fears about safety can affect a student's ability to learn.

The need for self-protection often increases the risks of violence.

When teachers must spend time dealing with violent behavior, they have less time to teach.

Money spent for safety measures and equipment could better be used to improve educational facilities.

Violence affects the families both of victims and of those who commit violence.

Chapter 4

The Effects of School Violence

Darien had a pretty good idea of who carried weapons at his

DARIEN, AGE 16

school. He hoped that no one would ever get hurt. However, he knew that terrible violence had occurred in unlikely places.

Darien was only a sophomore. Already, it was becoming harder to study. He couldn't concentrate on his classes. He felt like he spent much of his time waiting for something to happen. How could he stand to stay in school for another two years? Darien knew that he was old enough to get certain jobs. He wondered if it would be better to quit school and go to work. He hated to quit, but he didn't think he was learning much. Since he wasn't learning, anyway, he felt he might as well be away from school and feel safer.

The Burden of Fear

Physical injuries and deaths are the most obvious effects of violence. Violence also affects people emotionally.

When school becomes a place to dread, students may begin to skip it. Around 160,000 students miss class nationwide each day because they are afraid of physical harm. Many of those who do go are worried about injury from violence at school. Yet students need to be in school to learn.

The threat of any kind of violence can affect learning. Even motivated students may feel depressed when they are worried about being bullied or hurt. Students may not be safe, even if they don't intend to get involved in violence. It's hard for students to learn when they are worried about just making it through the day. They might feel like no one cares.

Perhaps the worst effect of fear is the things some students do to protect themselves. They may begin to carry a blade or a gun. Most students who carry a gun say they do it for self-protection. The more guns there are in school, for whatever reason, the greater the chance that someone will get hurt. The reality is that students really don't make themselves safer by carrying a weapon to school.

Violence at School

Jane's father had a collection of handguns in a locked

JANE, AGE 17

cabinet. She knew where the key was kept. She had often seen her father putting away the guns after cleaning them.

One evening when her parents were gone, Jane decided to borrow a gun. She thought that she might feel safer at school if she had a weapon. She packed it in her purse in case she needed it. Her father never noticed that the gun was missing.

A Changing Role for Teachers

Violence affects teachers, too. There are more than 2.5 million public school teachers in the United States. Every month, 5,000 are attacked. It's a small number—far below 1 percent of the total number of teachers. Violence, however, does happen to them. Many good teachers have left their profession. Teachers quit for many reasons. They may have left because they are afraid of the violence. They may be tired of the safety measures. Teachers have less time to teach if they must deal with violence. For example, say a teacher spends one hour a week disciplining a bully. That's five hours a week not used for teaching.

The Cost of Preventing School Violence

The effects of school violence can be measured in dollars and cents. Teachers and courses are being added to cover violence prevention as well as to cope with the effects of violence. When deaths occur as a result of violence, special counselors are brought in to help the survivors. These things cost extra money.

Schools across the country are spending more money on safety measures such as metal detectors. School buildings are being changed to make them safer. Full-time security guards are being hired. These things also cost extra money. However, they cannot guarantee students' safety.

The money that is spent on preventing school violence might be used to hire more teachers. It could be used to offer students a greater variety of classes. More and better computer labs could be installed. Extracurricular activities such as sports teams or musical options might be more varied. Money could be spent on activities that promote connections among students.

Paying attention to academics and to social and emotional needs and skills pays off for many schools. When students are connected to teachers and each other, their mental and emotional health improve.

The Effect of Violence on Families

School violence has many different victims, including family members. Families may feel hurt when a member is bullied. They feel sad or angry when something belonging to their teen is stolen. If a teen is hurt or killed, the family's grief is overwhelming.

FAST FACT

In 17 of the 50 United States, parents can be held responsible for the actions of their children.

The family of a violent teen also suffers. Parents, brothers, and sisters may spend years wondering what they did wrong. They may feel responsible for the actions of their child, brother, or sister. They may never stop wondering, "If only I had . . . ." A family may feel guilty and responsible if their teen stole something. They may have these feelings if the principal calls to say their teen spray-painted a school wall.

When a teen physically harms someone, life for the rest of the family often is changed forever. Family members may have to live with accusations and judgments from both acquaintances and strangers. Long after the violence has occurred, they may have to deal with attention from the media. Family members of violent teens sometimes find it necessary to move to a different community. They may feel that they must start over in a new location to get away from the attention. Not all families can or want to do this.

Points to Consider

Has fear affected any students you know? What happened?

How do you show your feelings when you are mad or angry at school? Does that hurt you or others? Explain.

How would you feel if one of your family members were a victim of violence at school?

Do you feel safe at school? Why or why not?

If schools had no problem with violence, how would they be different?

Chapter
Overview

Warning signs can help people recognize and stop violence before it happens.

Some schools offer classes in conflict resolution and provide peer mediation.

Schools can make physical changes to decrease the chance of violent activity.

Preventing violence is not only up to students. Caring adults can do many things to help.

Private and government programs help youth in conflict.

Chapter 5
Moving Ahead With Hope

It helps to know that schools are safe. Many efforts are making schools even safer. Preventing or limiting the conditions that lead to violence are the most effective ways to reduce school violence. As violence in schools decreases, learning and teaching become easier. Students who feel less afraid can think about friendships, extracurricular activities, and their education. Students and teachers alike feel less stress, because dangerous conflicts aren't as likely.

One day, Felice heard a group of boys at school talking. They were discussing who they would kill if they could. Felice told Ms. Markham, her homeroom teacher. "I didn't know if I should say anything," she explained. "They kind of scare me." Ms. Markham assured Felice that no one would know she had said something.

Ms. Markham told the police. The boys' parents allowed the police to search their homes. The school let the police look through the boys' lockers. There was nothing out of the ordinary. It appeared the boys had been just talking. Ms. Markham told Felice later, "Thank you for telling me. It doesn't matter that nothing happened. It's better to act as if something were wrong and then find out nothing is. I'm glad you felt you could trust me."

Sensitivity to Potential Danger

One way to prevent possible violence in school is to recognize warning signs. Everyone at school can watch for such signs. The signs may be easier to see in some people than in others. However, many people who commit violent acts behave in similar ways.

Sometimes people show warning signs but do not become violent. For example, maybe a student did poorly on a test and doesn't feel like talking about it. The student seems withdrawn but probably won't hurt someone. Still, someone you know may have several of the following signs over a period of time. If so, tell a responsible, trusted adult right away.

Withdrawing from others. Young people may feel depressed, rejected, or injured. They may lack confidence and keep away from other people.

Being bored with school or feeling inferior because of not doing well. Young people may feel no one cares about them.

Having angry outbursts over small problems. When angry, young people become less accepting of those who are different.

Being in a gang or having a desire to deal drugs. Gang members or drug dealers often carry guns or other weapons.

Committing theft or vandalism. Young people who commit small acts of violence may move on to deadlier violence.

Making threats or plans to hurt someone. Tell someone right away who can prevent such a person from committing dangerous acts.

Having weapons. Tell a responsible, trusted adult if you know of someone who carries weapons of any kind.

Here are ways you can help reduce violence and be a peacemaker:

Introduce yourself every week to one student you don't know yet.

Ask the school newspaper to write stories on violence prevention at school.

Ask school clubs to adopt antiviolence slogans or themes.

Don't keep quiet about kids who carry weapons.

Tell school authorities right away about any crime at school.

Tell a teacher or counselor about students' suspicious talk.

Conflict Resolution Programs

An even better solution to prevent violence of all kinds is to learn conflict resolution. Many schools offer programs for this. Students learn to communicate calmly and act peacefully. For example, students may be encouraged to identify a problem and ways to solve it. They may be asked to consider the outcomes of violence. They may answer the question, "Will my striking back improve the situation?"

In conflict resolution programs, students learn to say how they feel. For example, some students feel uncomfortable showing joy, fear, or sadness. If someone can help students identify that feeling, they may be more likely to share it. As students learn about their own feelings, they also learn empathy. That is, they try to understand how others may feel.

"Empathy is the ability to see through someone else's eyes, to hear through someone else's ears, and feel through someone else's heart."
—Alfred Adler, psychiatrist

Peer Mediation

A positive way to avoid violence in schools is through peer mediation. Students receive special training to act as a mediator, or go-between, for others. When students have an argument, they can get together with one or more mediators. The mediators help them to talk things out and move away from anger to focus on facts. After hearing both sides, mediators help the students resolve their own problems. The parties may be asked to sign an agreement. In it, they state that they will try their best for a peaceful follow-through.

Mediation gives students good alternatives to violence. Students like to know they are in charge of their own problems. Compromise and listening to one another can have positive outcomes. The goal of mediation is not to make the parties become friends. The goal is to give them a chance to talk about differences and make a productive change.

Changes at School

Beyond teaching conflict resolution and mediation, schools can make other additions or changes that might help reduce violence. For example, some schools provide more varied opportunities for classes and after-school activities. This gives more students the chance to get involved and to feel less alone.

Different physical setups at schools may make a difference. For instance, smaller schools or classes let teachers give students more attention. Schools can adjust schedules to reduce the number of students in hallways at the same time. Lunch breaks can be shifted so that smaller groups eat together. Schools can close the school campus during lunch periods to reduce the chances for outside trouble.

Some people believe that school uniforms reduce violence in schools. Uniforms may eliminate both competition over clothing and thefts of prized articles of clothing.

Steps Adults Can Take

Teens are not the only poeple who can stop violence in schools. Parents and other caring adults play a key role. Adults can teach nonviolent values and set an example of living by those values. Adults can teach that conflict is a normal part of life. They can show that not every conflict must have a winner and a loser. Caring adults can teach that real heroes don't use violence. Instead, real heroes avoid violence and are concerned about others.

Myth: Young children can't learn to prevent violence.

Fact: The most effective violence prevention training begins when children are young and continues as they mature.

By spending time with the kids they know, adults give the children a sense of importance. Adults and children can share activities involving TV, films, and video games. This allows parents or other adults to choose healthy programs or games for their children.

Adults can do other things to reduce violence. First, they can help keep guns out of the hands of their own and others' children. They can lock guns securely. They can use trigger guards and store the ammunition away from guns. Second, adults can ask questions of school officials. For example, they can find out what schools do when they need to call but can't reach parents. Third, caring adults can work together to influence school policies about violence, weapons, and visitors.

Private and Government Efforts to Reduce Violence

Private and government organizations are working to reduce school violence. Several examples are listed below. As such programs succeed, they may be models for similar programs in other places.

Minnesota's Make the Peace campaign reminds students that they are responsible to reduce violence. Also, students are encouraged to promote peace with their everyday words and actions.

Arizona's PeaceBuilders teaches students to encourage people, avoid insults, and seek out wise friends. Students learn to recognize when they hurt others and how to right those hurts.

Seattle's Committee for Children offers a program called Second Step. It teaches violence prevention to children as young as age 4.

A U.S. government program called Safe and Drug-Free Schools trains schools to increase safety. The program also supports Internet resources for help in opposing school violence.

The U.S. government has given 50 cities $300 million to prevent school violence. The money will finance training for teachers, afterschool programs, and more mental health professionals for schools. The program will help pay for security equipment such as metal detectors.

Points to Consider

Would you like to be a peer mediator? Why or why not?

Which adults do you look up to in your life? Why?

Which adult would you feel comfortable talking to if you heard a student making threats? Why?

Do you think school uniforms would cut down on violence? Why or why not?

Chapter Overview

People can learn to handle the fear of violence in school.

Showing respect by not starting or repeating insults and rumors may lead others to respect you.

You can deal with bullying by avoiding the person, talking it out, or reporting possession of weapons.

Being assertive can help you avoid conflict.

You can do many things to reduce violence, including letting people know you don't believe violence is acceptable.

Chapter 6

Making the Peace

Everyone hopes that school violence will decrease. Students and teachers alike want to get on with learning without the fear of violence. You can handle the fear while remaining in touch with friends and fellow students. You can help make schools even safer than they already are.

Giving Basic Respect

When you show respect for others, you help reduce violence. A good way to do this is to treat others the way you want to be treated.

Have you ever been insulted in school? Maybe you have insulted others. Even if someone isn't insulted directly, the target of the insult often hears someone else repeat it. Insults can lead to a spiral of negative feelings, which could lead to a violent confrontation. By not making or repeating insults, you show respect for others and help stop violent confrontations.

Starting or repeating rumors shows a lack of respect for others. The facts in these rumors may be true to some extent. However, the negative information still can cause hard feelings. Refusing to start or repeat rumors can limit the chance of angry flare-ups. This refusal also shows respect. If people know that you don't want to hear or repeat rumors, they may stop spreading them, too.

Dealing With Peer Pressure

Concern about what peers think can provoke confrontations at school. For instance, someone who is embarrassed may act angry to impress those who witnessed the embarassing event. The main concern may be to avoid looking afraid. However, *not* initiating violence shows self-respect. Avoiding violence usually takes more strength than behaving violently does. Looking like a smart, self-respecting person is better than trying to avoid looking weak.

Your friends may want you to participate in violent behavior. If so, you can try to get them to think about what they are doing. If they still want you to do something violent, maybe it's time to choose different friends. That can be a hard choice to make, but it is better for you.

Dealing With a Bully

Sometimes the problem of being bullied may go away on its own. However, ignoring the problem often can make it worse. At times it is best to avoid the bully. This may give you time to think of a way to talk it out. Then the bully may decide you are not someone to pick on.

Be firm but kind if you can't avoid the bully. Don't put the bully down. This will increase your dignity. That means you know you are worth being treated kindly yourself.

You may fear the bully is armed with a gun or knife. In that case, tell a teacher, counselor, or school safety person. It's not safe to confront a person who has a weapon.

Some schools have created policies of not tolerating any bullying. The students and teachers learn to step in and deal with any bullying behavior they see.

Here is a five-step method to react assertively.

1. **Stop:** Take time to calm down. Take a breath to relax.

2. **Think:** Try to decide why you or the other person might be angry.

3. **Talk:** Calmly say what you want or need. Focus on your feelings. Don't accuse the other person. For example, don't say, "You always call me names." Instead, you could say, "When you call me names, I feel confused, because I thought we were friends."

4. **Listen:** Ask what the other person feels, wants, thinks, or needs.

5. **Act:** Figure out how to make things right for everyone. Figure out a way that both you and the other person can walk away proudly.

Communicating Assertively

Violent behavior is often a reaction to something. For instance, someone may make a thoughtless statement. The other person may react angrily rather than communicating his or her confusion about the statement. The angry response may make the first person angry. When people communicate rather than react, the chances for peace are greater.

Kendra was angry. She knew that her sister Ginny had

borrowed her favorite blue sweater. Ginny was always taking Kendra's clothes without asking. Ginny wasn't home, but Kendra wanted her sweater back. She went to Ginny's dresser to get it.

Then Kendra decided to wait. She remembered her agreement with Ginny. They would stay out of each other's stuff unless given permission.

When Ginny got home, Kendra had cooled off. Kendra was assertive with Ginny and did not put her down. She calmly said, "I can't find my blue sweater. Do you have it?" Ginny admitted that she had taken the sweater without asking. Kendra said, "When you take my things without asking, I get mad. Please ask me before you take my stuff."

"I'm really sorry," Ginny said. "Believe me, I'll never do it again."

Assertiveness helps people to communicate well. If you respond clearly to someone, that person can understand you better. You can find out more about the problem. You might be able to suggest alternatives that will lead to a peaceful outcome. For example, Kendra did not just accuse her sister or go through her sister's stuff. She respected their agreement. She took time to cool off. Then she could communicate assertively about her sweater.

Assertive people are honest about their feelings. They stand up for their rights and respect themselves. They express their feelings and beliefs while respecting others. They are relaxed yet firm in their behavior. They understand it is a sign of strength to talk honestly about fears and other feelings. People who are assertive increase their chances of feeling good about themselves.

To communicate assertively, sit up or stand up straight. Usually, it's best to look the other person in the eyes. Speak calmly, without accusing the other person. Being calm increases the chances for peace. The chart may help you to determine how assertive you are.

Measure Your Assertiveness

Read items 1–13 below. Following each item, circle the number that best describes you. Use this rating scale as you circle the numbers.

1 = Never   2 = Rarely   3 = Sometimes   4 = Usually   5 = Always

1.	I do my own thinking and make my own decisions.	1 2 3 4 5
2.	I freely express my feelings and beliefs.	1 2 3 4 5
3.	I accept responsibility for my behavior.	1 2 3 4 5
4.	I make decisions and accept the consequences.	1 2 3 4 5
5.	When I need help, I ask others to help me.	1 2 3 4 5
6.	When at fault, I apologize.	1 2 3 4 5
7.	When confused, I ask for explanation.	1 2 3 4 5
8.	When someone is annoying me, I ask that person to stop.	1 2 3 4 5
9.	When treated unfairly or disrespectfully, I object.	1 2 3 4 5
10.	When I am interrupted, I politely comment on the interruption and then finish what I am saying.	1 2 3 4 5
11.	If friends invite me to do something that I really don't want to do, I turn down the request.	1 2 3 4 5
12.	When someone criticizes me, I listen to the criticism without being defensive.	1 2 3 4 5
13.	If I am jealous or envious, I explore the reasons for my feelings. Then I look for other ways to increase my self-confidence.	1 2 3 4 5

Total your score. The higher your score, the greater your level of assertive behavior.

Helping Make the Peace

It's not always easy to be a peacemaker. Here are some ideas to cope with fear and help reduce violence in your school. You may think of other ideas of your own.

Tell people that you think violence is not acceptable. Suggest that there are other ways to solve problems.

Introduce new students to your friends and other people you know. Being connected to other people is one of the best ways to avoid violence.

Don't carry weapons.

Cut down on the amount of violence you watch or listen to.

Control yourself because you can't control others.

Work out your arguments or walk away from them.

Start a peace pledge campaign. Have students sign an agreement to solve problems without using violence.

Don't spread racism, sexism, and other types of hate.

Become a peer counselor to help classmates who need support.

Help organize a school assembly to talk about peaceful compromise.

Work with teachers and counselors. Together develop a safe way to report threats, possession of weapons or drugs, gang activity, or vandalism.

Before the shooting in Littleton, the Colorado legislature was about to approve a law allowing concealed handguns. However, after the killings, the bill was pulled from consideration.

Be a mentor or role model for a younger student. Ask yourself if you ever do anything you would not want to see on the evening news.

Write to lawmakers about stricter gun control laws. Ask friends and family members to join you.

Start a school crime watch to help keep an eye on hallways and parking lots.

Take threats seriously. They may be a cry for help.

Help your school create zero tolerance for bullying. Have students and teachers pledge to be a part of the caring majority. Those people will step in and help stop any bullying behaviors they see.

Points to Consider

How can you deal with fear at school?

How is being treated with respect different from being treated disrespectfully?

Who are some peacemakers you know?

Do you think it's easier for adults or for teens to communicate assertively? Why?

Do you think you could be a role model? Why or why not?

Glossary

assault (uh-SAWLT)—harming someone physically

assertiveness (uh-SUR-tiv-nuhss)—self-confidence and the ability to stand up for one's own rights

copycat violence (COP-ee-kat VYE-uh-luhnss)—violence that appears to be copied from someone else's violent acts

desensitize (dee-SEN-suh-tize)—to make something or someone less easily affected by something; some programs on television may desensitize people to violence.

escalate (ESS-kuh-late)—to increase, enlarge, or grow stronger

homicide (HOM-muh-side)—the killing of someone; murder

media (MEE-dee-uh)—mass communication; television, radio, newspapers, magazines, video games, and advertising are all part of the media.

peer mediation (PEER mee-dee-AY-shuhn)—a process in which a third student helps two or more students settle a conflict peacefully

mentor (MEN-tur)—a person who helps someone who is younger or less experienced

peer pressure (PEER PRESH-ur)—the pressure peers put on each other to behave a certain way; peer pressure can be negative or positive.

resilience (ri-ZIL-ee-uhnss)—the ability to resist the effects of violence

role model (ROHL MOD-uhl)—someone who sets a positive example for another person or other people

stimulate (STIM-yuh-late)—to encourage something or someone to develop or grow

vandalism (VAN-duhl-iz-uhm)—needless destruction or damage to other people's property

violence (VYE-uh-luhnss)—words or actions that hurt people or things that people care about

For More Information

Dudley, William. *Media Violence: Opposing Viewpoints.* San Diego: Greenhaven, 1999.

Edgar, Kathleen J. *Media Violence.* New York: Rosen, 1998.

Gedatus, Gus. *Violence in the Media.* Mankato, MN: Capstone Press, 2000.

Guernsey, JoAnn Bren. *Youth Violence: An American Epidemic?* Minneapolis: Lerner, 1996.

Peacock, Judith. *Anger Management.* Mankato, MN: Capstone Press, 2000.

Useful Addresses and Internet Sites

Boys Town
The Village of Boys Town
Boys Town, Nebraska 68010
Hot line phone: 1-800-448-3000
Hot line e-mail: Hotline@boystown.org

Center for Violence and Injury Prevention
Education Development Center, Inc.
55 Chapel Street
Newton, MA 02158

National Crime Prevention Council
1700 K Street Northwest, 2d Floor
Washington, DC 20006-3817
www.ncpc.org/2schvio.htm

National Institute for Dispute Resolution
1726 M Street Northwest, Suite 500
Washington, DC 20036-4502

Violence Prevention Project
1010 Massachusetts Avenue
Boston, MA 02118

Family Education.Com
www.familyeducation.com/topic/front/
    0,1156,1-2179,00.htm
Quizzes, polls, and other information on
violence at school

United States Department of Justice—Justice
for Kids and Youth
www.usdoj.gov/kidspage/getinvolved
Information and links on gangs, drugs, abuse,
after-school programs, and getting involved

The Why Files—School Violence
www.whyfiles.news.wisc.edu/
    065school_violence
Information on school shootings, and gun
control, and links to other sites

Youth Crime Watch
www.ycwa.org
Helps teens work to reduce crime and drugs at
school and in the community

Index

abuse, 25
accusations, 9, 11, 36, 53–54
adults, 41, 44–45
alcohol, 16, 26
assault, 16
assertiveness, 52, 53–55

bullying, 7, 8, 17, 23, 25
    dealing with, 33, 51, 58

Columbine High School, 6, 8, 18, 22, 58
Committee for Children, 46
communication, 52–55
compromise, 43
conflict resolution programs, 21, 42, 44
copycat violence, 22
counselors, 34, 42, 46, 51
cowards, 25, 27
crowded schools, 23

drugs, 16, 26, 27, 41, 57

empathy, 42, 43

families, 35–36, 44–45
fear, 26, 32, 49, 56. *See also* feelings
    afraid
feelings
    afraid, 6, 7, 16, 19, 24, 31–32, 33.
        See also fear
    angry, 11, 21, 24, 26, 52, 53

fighting, 5, 9, 12, 22. *See also* physical violence
    walking away from, 25, 27
fitting in, 21
friends. *See* peer mediation; peer pressure

gangs, 41, 57
government organizations, 46, 47
graffiti, 10
guns, 10, 24, 27, 32, 33, 41, 45, 51
    availability of, 23–24

hitting, 24. *See also* physical violence
homicides, 5, 6, 7, 10, 17–18, 32, 34

impulse, acting on, 8
injuries, 5, 32
insults, 7, 8, 9, 50. *See also* verbal violence

judgments, 36

killings. *See* homicides
knives, 10, 51

listening, 43

Make the Peace, 46
media, 16, 27–28, 36, 42, 57, 58
mediation, 43
metal detectors, 34, 47
murder. *See* homicides
myths, 7, 28, 45

Index continued

nonviolent values, 44

PeaceBuilders, 46
peacemakers, 42, 56–58
peer mediation, 43, 57
peer pressure, 22, 24, 50–51
physical violence, 7, 8, 9, 15, 16, 25.
    See also fighting; hitting
portable classrooms, 23
preventing violence, 39, 40–41, 56–58
private organizations, 46
punishment, 24, 25

resilience, 25
respect, 49–50
role models, 21, 25, 44–45
rumors, 7, 11, 12, 50

Safe and Drug-Free Schools, 46
safety measures, 34, 39
school uniforms, 44
Second Step, 46
security guards, 34
self-esteem, 7, 8, 21, 25
self-protection, 24, 32, 33
sexual violence, 27
skipping school, 32
stabbings, 15
staying calm, 42, 52, 54
stress, 39
switchblades, 10, 15, 32

teachers, 9, 23, 33, 34–35, 39, 42, 47,
    49, 51
theft, 5, 7, 9, 15, 16, 41
threats, 7, 8, 9, 11, 12, 41

values, 44
vandalism, 5, 7, 9–10, 16, 41, 57
verbal violence, 6–7, 8. *See also*
    insults; yelling
violence at home, 25
violence at school
    causes of, 7, 12, 21–29
    contributing to, 11, 12, 42, 50
    cost of preventing, 34–35
    definition of, 7
    effects of, 10, 31–37
    history of, 15–19
    types of, 5–13
    preventing, 39, 40–41, 42–43,
    49–58
    recent occurrences of, 6, 17–18
    reporting, 9, 10, 42, 57

warning signs, 40–41
weapons, 7, 10, 15, 16, 17, 23, 24, 27,
    31, 32, 33, 41, 42, 45, 51, 57

yelling, 24. *See also* verbal violence